Journey Three

A collection of images from Travel Photographer of the Year

Imagos – The Photographers' Press

Publisher/Editor/Author – Chris Coe
Editor/Author – Karen Coe
Designer – Terry Steeley

First published by
Travel Photographer of the Year
20 Yew Tree Courtyard, Earl Soham, Suffolk IP13 7SG, UK.
www.tpoty.com

First edition published in 2010
ISBN 9780954939632

Reproduced, printed and bound by Connekt Colour, Berkhamstead, HP4 1EH, UK
Designed by Iridius Limited, Banbury, Oxfordshire OX16 9PA, UK

Front cover photograph: Holi festival, India. Poras Chaudhary, India

Frontispiece photograph: Young boy tries to catch a falling kite on the
River Ganges in Varanasi, India. David duChemin, Canada

Back cover photographs (clockwise from top left):
Irishman, New York, USA. Lasse Damgaard, Denmark
Emperor Penguin chicks in creche, Snow Hill Island, Weddell
Sea, Antarctica. Daisy Gilardini, Switzerland
Nomad girl, Amdo, Tibet. Jean-Claude Louis, USA
People watching wrestling match, Cheennj Fair, Shimla,
Himachal Pradesh, India. Poras Chaudhary, India
Ground Zero, New York, USA. Massimo Cristaldi, Italy
Theystareykir Terma Area, Fumarole, Iceland. Sergey Rumyantsev, Russia
Aspen Trees, Francis Lake, British Columbia, Canada. Tree trunks
lit by car headlights. Darwin Wiggett, Canada

New York, USA. Katherine Keates, Canada

CONTENTS

Journey Three is the third collection of images in the Travel Photographer of the Year series. It contains the winning images from the 2009, 2008 and 2007 awards, plus a few other great images of note. There will never be enough pages to include all the photographs that we'd like to, but even so the sheer diversity of subject matter is again startling.

One of the great joys of travel photography is that we all see the world differently and differing things inspire our photography. Journey Three depicts our world through the work of talented, inspiring photographers from across the continents. They've captured moments from a rapidly changing planet. There's beauty, of course, but not just that. Man's ability to enhance or destroy this unique planet is also evident in these photographs. This book is a running commentary on our varied lifestyles, cultures, celebrations and disasters; the worst and the best of humanity.

Our journey goes beyond man and our impact on earth. You'll also find the natural world in abundance. Landscapes at their most beautiful and extreme, often transient moments sculpted by light and weather. And every form of life, from the largest mammals to the smallest, through the spectrum of birds, insects, flora and fauna in all their majesty. But turn the pages and enjoy discovering for yourself.

Novice monk, Punakha, Bhutan. Manuel Librodo Jnr., Philippines

Underlying it all is a shared passion for the still image. Beautiful photography will never cease to captivate, perhaps because it brings together reality, creativity and imagination. Perhaps because it requires a vision and patience which many of us don't possess, or choose not to cultivate. For every image in this book, the photographer had to take a journey; sometimes just a short distance, sometimes a more challenging expedition. If their images have succeeded they will take you effortlessly on these same journeys through their images.

Since the Travel Photographer of the Year awards started in 2003, the world of photography has undergone a major transformation. More than a century of capturing images using silver halide has been rapidly overtaken by a new world of pixels and megabytes. Have these changes led to better imagery? Arguably no. Have they made photography more accessible? Definitely yes, and this must be a good thing, as new generations discover photography and are inspired to take their own pictures.

Photography has never been all about equipment, but it always has been and always will be all about the image. The technology debate was erroneous. Technological changes only allow more of us to take pictures more easily. They don't make us better photographers. It's still the combination of light and photographic craft which permits us to make, rather than take, images which have the power to enthrall, intrigue, engage, move, stimulate and motivate.

Playfighting hippos, Zambia. Marsel van Oosten, Netherlands

Through the awards we've been privileged to observe the influence of new technology on image making and it has never been more apparent - as we've seen each year's entries over this period of change - that the camera is simply a tool, and no substitute for skill and vision. In 2009 we saw the first, and mostly unsuccessful, attempts from entrants to master HDR image capture. Perhaps this will prove to be yet another 'red herring' in relation to great photography as it diverts the photographer from the need to think about their most important photographic tool - light. Only time will tell.

Travel and photography now share a common characteristic; they are both easily accessible journeys to embark upon. Yet it is frequently true that the best journeys require more effort, and challenge us the most. If you look at the images on these pages and think you could do that, or do better, then do it! But don't underestimate the skills of these photographers. There are some remarkable stories behind many of the images, and we'll bring you the best of these in the future in another book.

As with all the Journey Portfolios, the featured photographers are not constrained by age or profession. The images were taken by people of all ages, and by amateur and professional photographers. Whether you aspire to be a similarly skillful photographer or simply enjoy taking this visual journey, you cannot fail to appreciate the talent, perseverance, creativity and imagination - and sometimes sheer luck - which have gone into their photography. So sit back, turn the pages and escape....

Enjoy the journey!

TRAVEL PHOTOGRAPHER OF THE YEAR 2009

Striking travel photography in a reportage style tells well crafted stories in Akash's winning portfolios. These go beyond simple observation and enter the lives of the people in his images in a vibrant and engaging way. His two sets of images each have a very different feel but both draw you into their very different stories.

Sponsors of this award:

Adobe, Harman Technology, Mountain Paradise, Lexar, Plastic Sandwich, Wacom

Ship breaking yard, Gaddani, Pakistan. G.M.B.Akash, Bangladesh

Ship breaking yard, Gaddani, Pakistan. G.M.B.Akash, Bangladesh

TRAVEL PHOTOGRAPHER OF THE YEAR 2009

G.M.B. Akash Bangladesh
Winner

Akash's passion for photography began in 1996. He attended the World Press Photo seminar in Dhaka for 3 years and graduated with a BA in Photojournalism. He has received more than 40 international awards from all around the world and his work has been featured in over 50 major international publications.

In 2002 he became the first Bangladeshi to be selected for the World Press Photo Joop Swart Masterclass in the Netherlands. In 2004 he received the Young Reporters Award from the Scope Photo Festival in Paris, again being the first Bangladeshi to receive the honour. In 2005 he was awarded Best of Show at the Center for Fine Art Photography's international competition in Colorado, USA. In 2006 he was awarded World Press Photo award and released his first book 'First Light'.

In 2007 he became the first Bangladeshi to be selected for the 30 Emerging Photographers (PDN 30) by Photo District News Magazine, USA. He won the 7th Vevey international photography grant from Switzerland in 2009.

Ship breaking yard, Gaddani, Pakistan. G.M.B.Akash, Bangladesh

Ship breaking yard, Gaddani, Pakistan. G.M.B.Akash, Bangladesh

Woman traveling on the locking system of a carriage, Bangladesh. G.M.B.Akash, Bangladesh

Helaluddin frequently travels like this on his day off from the plastic factory where he works. Dhaka, Bangladesh. G.M.B.Akash, Bangladesh

Even deep sleep is no problem during the commute. Dhaka, Bangladesh. G.M.B.Akash, Bangladesh

Going home at the end of the day. Dhaka, Bangladesh. G.M.B.Akash, Bangladesh

YOUNG TRAVEL PHOTOGRAPHER
OF THE YEAR 2009

A Place I Love: Unusually, the 2009 young winner's award was given to a portfolio which mixes black & white with colour imagery, in an entry showing interesting use of viewpoint. In the two images of people, 15 year old Courtney Krawec has captured both a thoughtfulness and the pure joy of a moment. Together with her other two images she has shown us the places she loves both illustratively and in terms of an emotional response from the people who make it special for her.

Sponsors of this award:

Adobe, Lexar, Photo Iconic, Rough Guides, Wacom

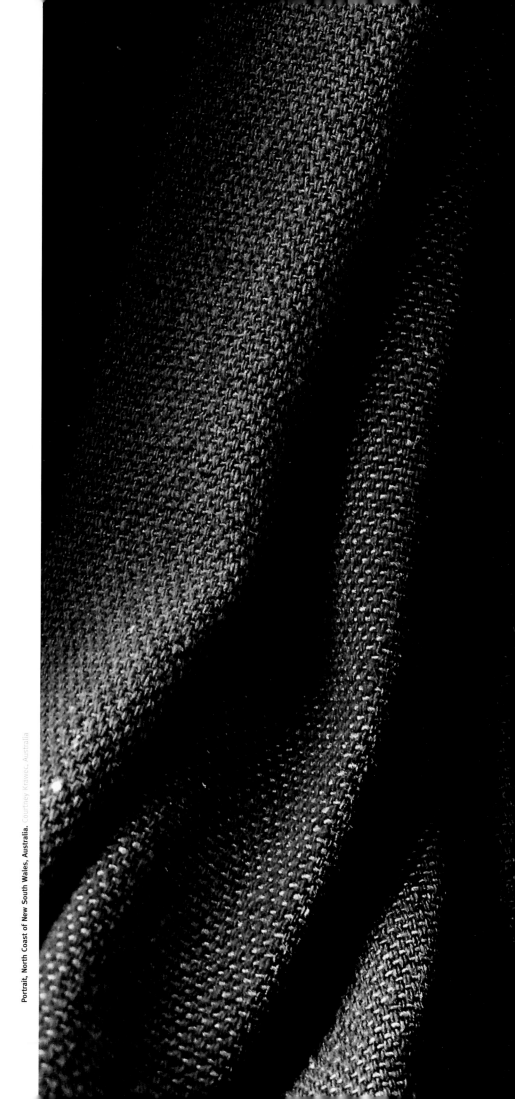

Portrait, North Coast of New South Wales, Australia. Courtney Krawec, Australia

Portrait, North Coast of New South Wales, Australia. Courtney Krawec, Australia

Forest, North Coast of New South Wales, Australia. Courtney Krawec, Australia

Starfish, North Coast of New South Wales, Australia. Courtney Krawec, Australia

YOUNG TRAVEL PHOTOGRAPHER OF THE YEAR 2009

Courtney Krawec Australia
Winner

15 year old Courtney Krawec first became interested in photography after visiting Peter Lik's photo gallery, in Noosa, Australia, four years ago, when she was just 11 years old. The colour and impact of Lik's photographs inspired her to pick up her own camera and begin capturing that elusive image that speaks to the viewer. She enjoys a wide variety of photographic styles and has recently become interested in fashion photography.

Young Travel Photographer of the Year is the fourth international award Courtney has received, giving her very real encouragement to pursue a career in photography.

PEOPLE OF THE WORLD PORTFOLIO 2009

Martin Edström's portfolio gives a real sense of the lives of these Cape Verde fishermen in a beautifully constructed and well told story. The images have an engaging atmosphere, which adds to his portrayal of the realism and harshness of their daily struggle.

Sponsors of this award:

Adobe, Intrepid Travel, Harman Technology, Jacobs Digital Photo & Video, Lee Filters, Lexar, Rough Guides, Wacom

Village on the cliffs, Santo Antao, Cape Verde. Martin Edström, Sweden

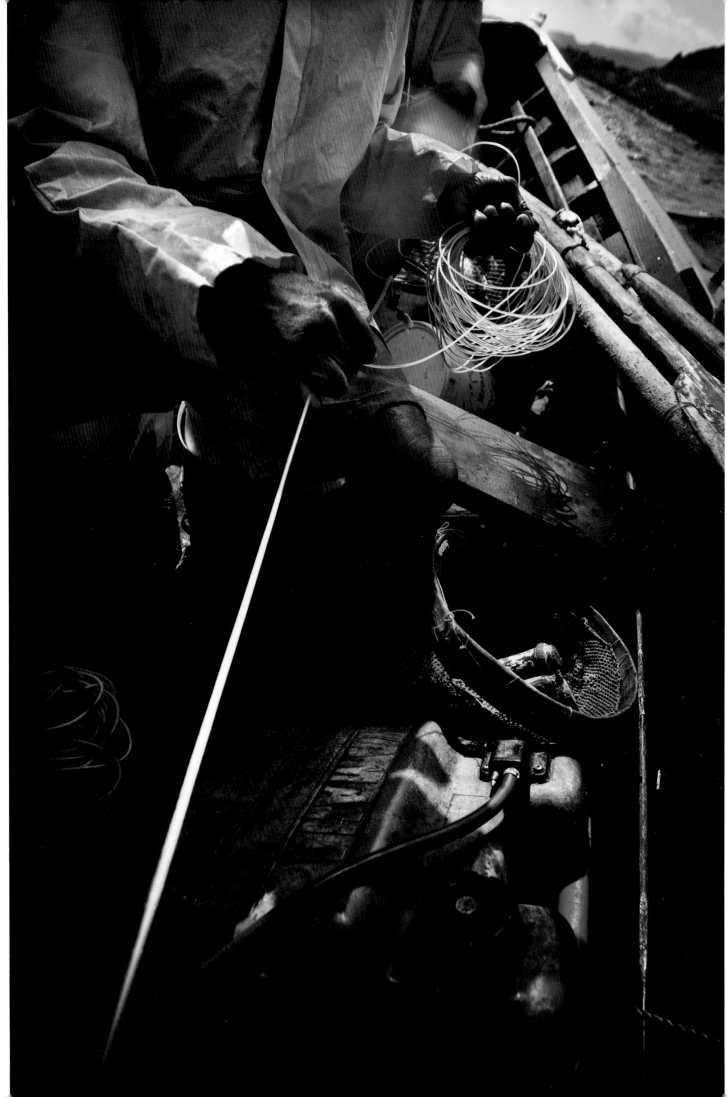

PEOPLE OF THE WORLD

Martin Edström Sweden
Winner

Martin started shooting with his grandfather's camera as a child, and became caught up in the world of pictures. His first-ever assignment was for a travel magazine, where his passion for travelling was combined with the will to write and photograph.

Now he focuses on documentary features and has worked with organisations such as the Red Cross and MSF as well as with several Swedish magazines and newspapers. Documentary projects about HIV/AIDS have taken him through large parts of Africa, producing images which have been exhibited at the Newseum in Washington D.C. In the summer of 2009 he started the documentary project Carpe Diem by following environmental and eco-tourism projects in the Amazon.

With a lifestyle on the road, working with travel and adventure comes naturally. Aside from freelancing as a photographer and writer, he studies journalism in Stockholm.

Far out in the Atlantic Ocean, Santo Antao, Cape Verde. Martin Edström, Sweden

Just out of Ponta so Sol, Santo Antao, Cape Verde. Martin Edström, Sweden

Cape Verde fishermen, 400 miles from home, Mamelles, Dakar, Senegal. Martin Edström, Sweden

Barber shop near the dargah (shrine) of the Sufi saint, Sheikh Nizamuddin Aulia, West Nizamuddin, New Delhi, India. Karoki Lewis, India/UK

PEOPLE OF THE WORLD

Karoki Lewis India/UK
Runner Up

Karoki's intimate images of daily life in New Delhi are enhanced by his interesting use of dual viewpoints, giving a wonderful insight into the ordinary.

Muslim prostrates in prayer as pilgrims gather, West Nizamuddin, New Delhi, India. Karoki Lewis, India/UK

Vegetable vendor in front of butcher's shop, Mehrauli, New Delhi, India. Karoki Lewis, India/UK

Living in a converted 14th century tomb, West Nizamuddin, New Delhi, India. Karoki Lewis, India/UK

Life in a traditional Miao village, Guizhou, China. Larry Louie, Canada

Life in a traditional Miao village, Guizhou, China. Larry Louie, Canada

PEOPLE OF THE WORLD

Larry Louie Canada
Highly Commended

Intriguing and captivating in their simplicity, Larry's images cleverly use interaction and non-interaction to great effect.

Dutch professor on his way to class, Amsterdam, Netherlands. Lasse Damgaard, Denmark

Irishman, New York, USA. Lasse Damgaard, Denmark

PEOPLE OF THE WORLD

Lasse Damgaard Denmark
Commended

Lasse has captured witty and engaging portraits of interesting characters with a lifetime of stories etched on their faces.

NATURAL WONDERS
PORTFOLIO 2009

The plight of the polar bears and their threatened habitat is currently highly topical. But rather than portray them as cute and cuddly, Craig Churchill's portfolio has a more gritty feel, much more in keeping with the harsh environment and the temperament of these impressive creatures.

Sponsors of this award:

Adobe, Intrepid Travel, Harman Technology, Jacobs Digital Photo & Video, Lee Filters, Lexar, NEC, Rough Guides

Polar bear, Svalbard, Norway. Craig Churchill, UK

Polar bears competing for flesh of dead fin whale, Svalbard, Norway. Craig Churchill, UK

NATURAL WONDERS

Craig Churchill UK
Winner

Craig Churchill was brought up in a rural north Oxfordshire village surrounded by large areas of open farmland. This, coupled with an exposure to his father's interest in wildlife, soon rubbed off and an interest in photography followed. An initial interest in photographing birds soon developed to include all aspects of the natural world and British wildlife in particular. An encounter with a family of foxes in 1988 led to his very first competition entry resulting in a runners-up prize in the Junior BBC Wildlife Photographer of the Year.

He has had work published in numerous publications and also has a number of wildlife organisations amongst his client list including English Nature, Greater London Authority and the Black Redstart Organisation.

Craig now strives to capture his subjects in new and interesting ways, introducing a fresh outlook on the natural world as opposed to traditional 'frame-filling' images.

Polar bear on fin whale carcass, Svalbard, Norway. Craig Churchill, UK

Polar bear feeding on rotting fin whale carcass, Svalbard, Norway. Craig Churchill, UK

Portrait of Emperor Penguin chick, Snow Hill Island, Weddell Sea, Antarctica. Daisy Gilardini, Switzerland

NATURAL WONDERS

Daisy Gilardini Switzerland
Runner Up

Stunningly simple and strikingly effective images.

Polar bear, Wapusk National Park, Manitoba, Canada. Daisy Gilardini, Switzerland

Fairy tern, Midway Atoll, Hawaii, USA. Daisy Gilardini, Switzerland

Emperor Penguin chicks in creche, Snow Hill Island, Weddell Sea, Antarctica. Daisy Gilardini, Switzerland

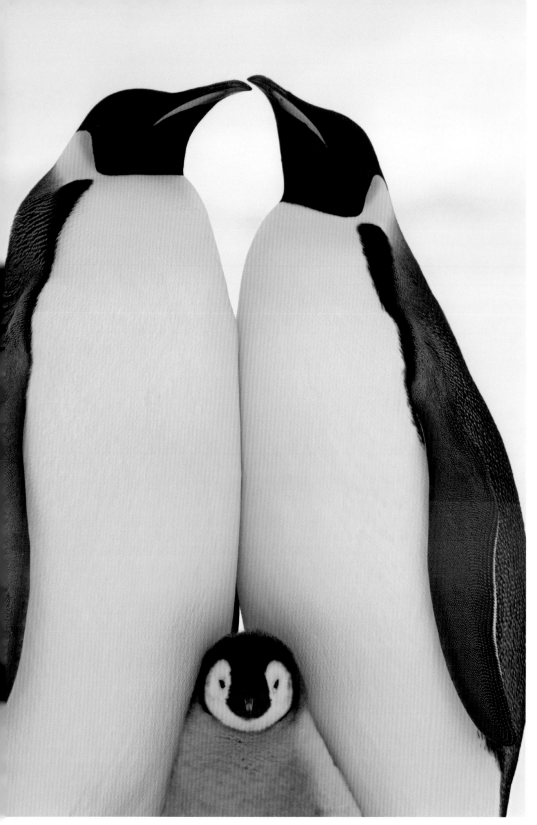

Emperor Penguin family, Antarctica. Sue Flood, UK

Emperor Penguins, Antarctica. Sue Flood, UK

NATURAL WONDERS

Sue Flood UK

Highly Commended

Sue's images are a charming and amusing portrayal of penguin adventures.

NATURAL WONDERS

Louis Montrose USA
Commended

Classic black and white landscapes full of tactile textures and tones.

Antelope Canyon, Arizona, USA. Louis Montrose, USA

South Coyote Buttes, Arizona, USA. Louis Montrose, USA

HOMELAND PORTFOLIO 2009

In most people's minds, India is associated with vibrant life and vivid colours. Poras Chaudhary's portfolio of his homeland is unmistakably India, capturing the essence of the upbeat country which attracts travellers, in an intriguing and intense set of images.

Sponsors of this award:

Adobe, Intrepid Travel, Harman Technology, Jacobs Digital Photo & Video, Lee Filters, Lexar, Rough Guides, Wacom

People watching wrestling match, Cheenni Fair, Shimla, Himachal Pradesh, India. Poras Chaudhary, India

Drying sarees, Kurukshetra, Haryana, India. Poras Chaudhary, India

Festival of Colours, Mathura, Uttar Pradesh, India. Poras Chaudhary, India

Last man standing, Holi festival, Mathura, Uttar Pradesh, India. Poras Chaudhary, India

HOMELAND

Poras Chaudhary India
Winner

Born in Kurukshetra, a small city of Northern India, Poras Chaudhary is a freelance photojournalist and a documentary photographer. Ever since he was a child, he has been intrigued by the visually striking moments, whether special for their colour, composition or just the moment's rarity in time.

His passion for photography began in 2005 when he started looking for a good camera and came across the work of Magnum photographers. Poras is a completely self-taught photographer. He is best known for his colour work and unique compositions. Having only started 'serious' photography in mid-2005, he has already won a number of internationally recognised awards.

Khirki village, New Delhi, India. Karoki Lewis, India/UK

Begumpur village, New Delhi, India. Karoki Lewis, India/UK

Emperor Bahiol Lodi's tomb, Chiragh Delhi village, New Delhi, India. Karoki Lewis, India/UK

HOMELAND

Karoki Lewis India/UK
Runner Up

These black and white images take you deep into a side of India which few tourists experience, to a very different homeland below the surface veneer.

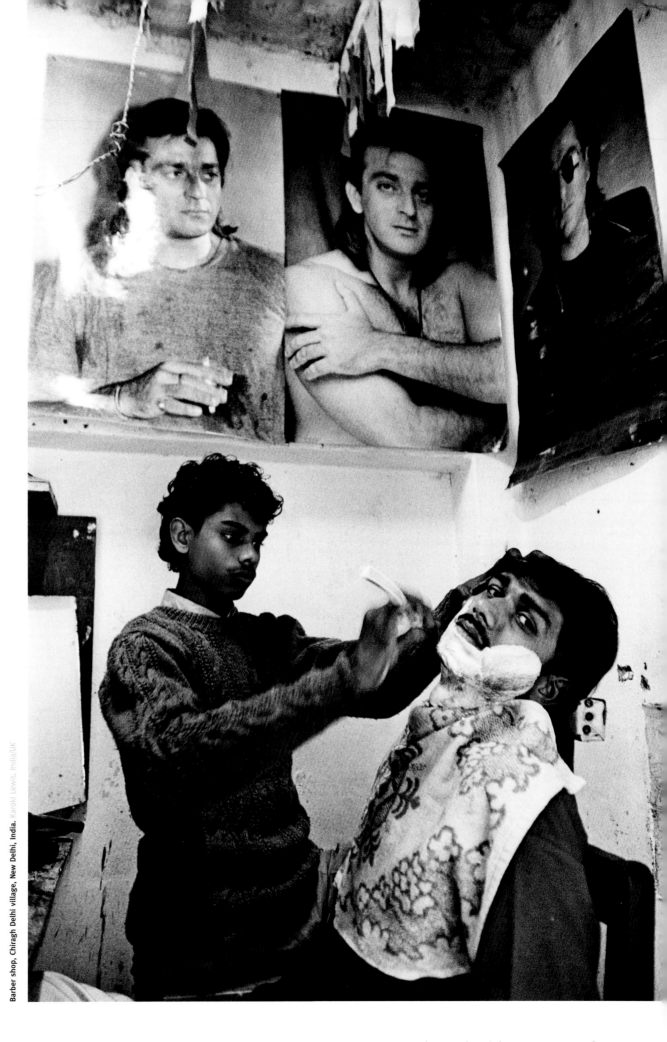

Barber shop, Chiragh Delhi village, New Delhi, India. Karoki Lewis, India/UK

HOMELAND

Craig Easton UK
Highly Commended

Craig's beautiful, almost monochromal, seascapes portray a
tranquil side to Britain's dramatic and varied coastline, giving
a real sense of solitude and escape.

Saint Mary's Lighthouse, Whitley Bay, England. Craig Easton, UK

The Small Isles after sunset from Ardnamurchan, Scotland. Craig Easton, UK

View of St. Paul's from the Millenium Bridge, London, England. Ron Tear, UK

Turbine Hall, Tate Modern, London, England. Ron Tear, UK

HOMELAND

Ron Tear UK

Commended

Details of a familiar London allow you to experience an
etherial view of one of this capital city's most visited areas.

ONE SHOT 2009

Festival, Fiesta & Celebration: Louis Montrose's ghostly and haunting portrayal of Mexico's El dia de los Muertos (the Day of the Dead), cleverly captured in black and white, gives a real sense of this macabre yet joyous celebration.

Sponsors of this award:

Adobe, Harman Technology, Jacobs Photo & Video, Lexar, Rough Guides

El dia de Los Muertos, Oaxaca, Mexico. Louis Montrose, USA

African dancer, Liberian National Peace & Cultural Festival. Jonathan Banks, UK

FESTIVAL, FIESTA & CELEBRATION

Louis Montrose USA
Winner

Lou Montrose was born in London, grew up in New York City, and has lived in southern California for many years. His engagement as a visual artist springs from a passion for creating and viewing images that began in childhood.

During a successful academic career in the humanities, he also wrote and taught about the history and cultural power of images. He now pursues his calling as a photographer full time,

working in a number of genres, including cityscape and street, environmental portrait and travel, and night photography.

He has a compelling interest in the power of photography to capture the vibrancy and diversity of human cultures, and values colour as an essential expressive and communicative medium. At the same time, he is deeply drawn to black and white photography.

FESTIVAL, FIESTA & CELEBRATION

Jonathan Banks UK
Runner Up

Subtle tones and an amazing sky enhance the splendour of this African dancer.

Arirang Mass Games, Pyong Yang, North Korea. Mark Edward Harris, USA

FESTIVAL, FIESTA & CELEBRATION

Mark Edward Harris USA
Highly Commended

Pomp, ceremony and military might come together in a strong composition, yet the uniformity is so strong that they look as if they could be toy soldiers.

FESTIVAL, FIESTA & CELEBRATION

Kieron Nelson Canada
Commended

A delightful and uplifting moment.

Miao girls, Changjiao, China. Kieron, Nelson, Canada

NEW TALENT 2009

Photo Essay – A Traveller's Tale: Taylor Weidman's photo essay captures the tragic story of Romanian orphans in striking imagery which conveys the sense of hopelessness and desperation in key elements of these people's lives. The story needs few, if any, words and the portfolio is well constructed to tell it.

Sponsors of this award:

Adobe, Jacobs Digital Photo & Video, Lexar, Linhof Studio, Mountain Paradise, Plastic Sandwich

Homeless family squatting in abandoned building, Bucharest, Romania. Taylor Weidman, USA

Homeless man with hands stained from huffing paint thinner, Bucharest, Romania. Taylor Weidman, USA

NEW TALENT

Taylor Weidman USA
Winner

Taylor Weidman's wanderlust has taken him all over the globe. Since completing a Master's degree in photography in early 2009, Taylor has produced projects on the electricity crisis in rural Africa, the homeless in Romania and the overcrowded prison system in the Philippines. Through his experiences, he has become a strong believer that compelling visual stories exist in every community.

Photo Essay
'Across from the Romanian Parliament in an old abandoned building, a group of homeless people and their families have begun squatting. The building has no heat or running water, and electricity is stolen from the city. None of the adults work. They have grown up orphaned on the streets – a result of the irresponsible and dangerous policies of the former Romanian leader Nicolae Ceaucescu. Now adults, they are starting families of their own, and, though they want better lives for their children, the children are facing many of the same problems their parents did.'

Squatter children, Bucharest, Romania. Taylor Weidman, USA

Orphan sniffing glue, Bucharest, Romania. Taylor Weidman, USA

Worker begins the destruction of another building with a homemade sledgehammer, Zibo, Shandong, China. Shelby Karns, USA

Old man interrupting soccer game in street, Barcelona, Spain. Douglas Ljungkvist, USA

NEW TALENT

Douglas Ljungkvist USA
Runner-Up

Douglas's well observed images showed how all age groups were enjoying life in Barcelona, a city he described as 'so well designed, dynamic, and vibrant'.

NEW TALENT

Shelby Karns USA
Highly Commended

Shelby's emotive portfolio graphically depicted the process in which, over just two days, a 15-acre Chinese village was reduced to rubble, against the wishes of its inhabitants.

NEW TALENT

Kym Morris Australia
Commended

A journey through Rajasthan showed Kym the very different world inhabited by the workers she photographed - a world she gave us a glimpse of with her portfolio.

Preparing dinner, Bei village, India. Kym Morris, Australia

FIRST SHOT 2009

Postcards from Anywhere: The First Shot category is for less experienced amateur photographers who are still learning their craft. The judges chose the five winners as entrants whose images show the potential to develop their photography and who will benefit from the tuition on offer as their prize. Five runner up entries were also chosen.

Sponsors of this award:
Adobe, Photo Iconic

Serengeti National Park, Tanzania. Jonathan Allen, UK

Patterns in the sand, Cable Beach, Broome, Western Australia. Mieke Boynton, Australia

POSTCARDS FROM ANYWHERE

Winners

Deb Hillerby UK
Jonathan Allen UK
Julie Ruck USA
Mieke Boynton Australia
Sheryll Sulit UK

Childhood dreams, Winnetka, Illinois, USA. Julie Ruck, USA

Hastings, UK. Sheryll Sulit, UK

Table for two, La Guarida restaurant, Centro Habana, Cuba. Deb Hillerby, UK

Eye of the Emirates, Sharjah, United Arab Emirates. Tareq Alhamrani, UAE

Teenagers flirting at sunset, Bali, Indonesia. Kevin Ummel, USA

Breckenridge, Colorado, USA. Louise Croak, UK

POSTCARDS FROM ANYWHERE

Runners Up

Charlotte Hedley UK

Deb Hillerby UK

Kevin Ummel USA

Louise Croak UK

Tareq Alhamrani UAE

Centro Habana, Cuba. Deb Hillerby, UK

Sheikh Lotfollah Mosque, Isfahan, Iran. Charlotte Hedley, UK

BEST SINGLE IMAGE
IN PORTFOLIO 2009

Each year there are many portfolio entries which don't win prizes but which contain outstanding individual images. In 2009 outstanding single images were chosen by the judging panel from all three portfolio categories, with further images of note awarded special mentions.

Sponsors of this award:

Adobe, Harman Technology, Jacobs Digital Photo & Video

Eye of humpback whale, Vava'u Islands, Kingdom of Tonga. Sue Flood, UK

Storm approaching haunted Sandwood Cottage, Cape Wrath, Scotland. Craig Easton, UK

NATURAL WONDERS

Sue Flood UK
Winner

A serenely beautiful and majestic image. Sue has captured the gentleness of this creature with fascinating detail provided by the war wounds and crabs.

HOMELAND

Craig Easton UK
Winner

Striking composition and a moment of incredible natural light come together to create Craig's stunning landscape.

PEOPLE OF THE WORLD

Johan Ensing Netherlands
Winner

A intriguing image notable for its unconventional composition and beautiful lighting. Johan has found a lovely balance between natural light and added flash.

Kevin Cozma Canada
Special Mention

Great fun image from an intriguing perspective.

Lung Liu Canada
Special Mention

At first glance, an ordinary scene - until you spot the face. Then Lung Liu's image becomes very powerful.

HOMELAND

Harald Mundt Germany
Special Mention

A everyday image of travel in Afghanistan comes together in Harald's image through careful positioning of the background elements to paint a picture and a portrait of life and travel.

After the fishing, Erhai Lake, Dali, China. Johan Ensing, Netherlands

Street scene, Kunduz, Afghanistan. Harald Mundt, Germany

Nephew sleeping, Lao Cai, Vietnam. Lung Liu, Canada

Young girl on swing, Takamatsu, Kagawa, Japan. Kevin Cozma, Canada

TRAVEL PHOTOGRAPHER
OF THE YEAR 2008

Clever use of light, both natural and artificial, make Darwin Wiggett's beautiful landscapes and details of nature a striking winner of the 2008 awards. They are a perfect illustration of how photography is all about light.

Sponsors of this award:

Adobe, Intrepid Travel, Lee Filters, Linhof & Studio, Plastic Sandwich

Abraham Lake, Kootenay Plains, Alberta, Canada. Ice formations in winter. Darwin Wiggett, Canada

TRAVEL PHOTOGRAPHER OF THE YEAR 2008

Darwin Wiggett Canada
Winner

Darwin Wiggett is one of Canada's most well known and published landscape, nature and travel photographers. He has had numerous books published including the best sellers 'Dances with Light - The Canadian Rockies' and 'How to Photograph the Canadian Rockies'. Darwin is also a columnist and contributor to 'Outdoor Photography Canada' magazine and former co-editor of Canada's 'Photo Life' magazine.

Darwin specialises in landscape, nature and travel photography in his home country of Canada. Although he loves international travel, Canada is so big and so full of opportunity that Darwin feels there is a lifetime of photographic work to be done there.

Abraham Lake, Kootenay Plains, Alberta, Canada. Ice formations in winter. Darwin Wiggett, Canada

Abraham Lake, Kootenay Plains, Alberta, Canada. Ice formations in winter. Darwin Wiggett, Canada

Abraham Lake, Kootenay Plains, Alberta, Canada. Ice formations in winter. Darwin Wiggett, Canada

Kootenay Plains – Canadian Rockies, Alberta, Canada. Limber pine lit by flashlight under the Northern Lights. Darwin Wiggett, Canada

Frenchman Beach Provincial Park, Vancouver Island, Canada. Stump lit by flashlight.
Darwin Wiggett, Canada

Red Rock Coulee, Alberta, Canada. Rock lit by flashlight.
Darwin Wiggett, Canada

Aspen Trees, Francis Lake, British Columbia, Canada. Tree trunks lit by car headlights. Darwin Wiggett, Canada

YOUNG TRAVEL PHOTOGRAPHER OF THE YEAR 2008

Journey: A shortlisted entrant on a number of previous occasions, 16 year old Daniel Rooney finally won the award of Young Travel Photographer of the Year in the last year before he becomes too old to be eligible. Over the years his photography has improved steadily and his winning portfolio shows a developing ability to observe and engage with his subjects.

Sponsors of this award:

Adobe, Iridius, Lexar, Photo Iconic, Plastic Sandwich, Wacom

Woman with incense sticks, A-Ma Temple, Macau, China. Daniel Rooney, UK

Portrait, Hanoi, Vietnam. Daniel Rooney, UK

Buddhist monk, Temple of Literature, Hanoi Vietnam.
Daniel Rooney, UK

YOUNG TRAVEL PHOTOGRAPHER OF THE YEAR 2008

Daniel Rooney UK
Winner

The son of a photographer, Daniel Rooney first became interested in photography in 2004, when he was given a Nikon Coolpix. He started by taking pictures in his local area and on holidays. In 2006 his parents took him out of school to travel around India, Singapore, Malaysia, Thailand, Vietnam and China for seven months and he bought a Nikon D70s to use on the trip.

The images of Steve McCurry inspired and influenced him during the trip, and he has also studied - and admires - the work of Michael Kenna.

16 year old Daniel hopes one day to become a professional photographer. His father's talent is clearly being passed on; Daniel's younger brother Jordan was Commended in the 2008 TPOTY awards.

Soldier looking at portrait of Chairman Mao, Beijing, China. Daniel Rooney, UK

LIFE PORTFOLIO 2008

For 2007 New Talent winner, Charlie Mahoney, the success continued with this gritty insight into the harsh life of two Irish brothers and their farm. A well told story and concise portfolio which is a worthy winner of the Life category.

Sponsors of this award:

Adobe, Intrepid Travel, Lee Filters, Lexar, TPOTY, Wacom

Farmers, County Cork, Ireland. Charlie Mahoney, USA

Farmers, County Cork, Ireland. Charlie Mahoney, USA

Farmers, County Cork, Ireland. Charlie Mahoney, USA

LIFE

Charlie Mahoney USA
Winner

Following a 15-year career in finance and investment, Charlie Mahoney completed a Master's in Photojournalism at the Universidat Autonoma de Barcelona in July 2006. The following month he began a three-month trip through Benin, Burkina Faso and Togo. He has subsequently travelled to St. Bart's in the French West Indies, Prague, Albania, Montenegro and Corfu, Greece.

In 2007 Charlie won the New Talent award in TPOTY.

Charlie especially likes to work on stories of human interest and has experience working in remote locations. He strongly believes that photojournalism can promote change by functioning as a witness and giving a voice to people who are powerless to tell their own stories.

Farmers, County Cork, Ireland. Charlie Mahoney, USA

LIFE

Tessa Bunney UK
Runner Up

Delicately observed cameos of Vietnamese women give
Tessa's images an endearing quality.

'Home work': domestic labour in the villages around Hanoi, Vietnam. Tessa Bunney, UK

'Home work': domestic labour in the villages around Hanoi, Vietnam.
Tessa Bunney, UK

'Home work': domestic labour in the villages around Hanoi, Vietnam.
Tessa Bunney, UK

Potter, Kerala, India. Mani Puthuran, India/UK

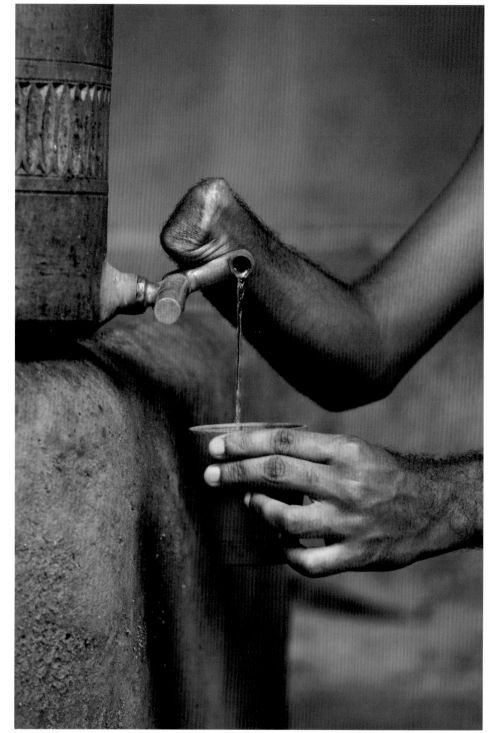

Waterseller, Kerala, India. Mani Puthuran, India/UK

Fisherman with Boats, Taghazhout, Morocco. Lachlan Millard, Australia

LIFE

Mani Puthuran India/UK
Highly Commended

Mani's intimate portraits of craftsmen and traders are all the stronger for the absence of colour and the clever use of narrow depth of field.

LIFE

Lachlan Millard Australia
Commended

An atmospheric portrayal of Moroccan life, shot in beautiful light.

Ladies at Mosque, Casablanca, Morocco. Lachlan Millard, Australia

CALL OF THE WILD
PORTFOLIO 2008

The portrayal in black and white adds to the icy feel of Andrew Peacock's portfolio of images which capture man's lure into some of the planet's most forbidding places. Unspoiled despite this invasion, the magnificence of the natural and wild landscape dwarfs man's presence and significance.

Sponsors of this award:

Adobe, Intrepid Travel, Lee Filters, Lexar, Plastic Sandwich, TPOTY, Wacom

Lone hiker in the view of Shreckhorn, above Grindlewald, Swiss Alps. Andrew Peacock, Australia

Below the summit ice mushroom on Aoraki/Mt Cook, Southern Alps New Zealand. Andrew Peacock, Australia

CALL OF THE WILD

Andrew Peacock Australia
Winner

Australia-based adventure and travel photographer Andrew Peacock first began to look seriously through a camera lens while working as a medical doctor on voluntary assignments in Nepal and India in 1996. An active climber, paddler and mountaineer, his work features in numerous Lonely Planet titles and has been published in a wide range of magazines.

When not enjoying life on the road Andrew lives on the beautiful Sunshine Coast of Queensland, Australia.

Icebergs in bay near Ilulissah, Greenland. Andrew Peacock, Australia

Mountaineers en route to climb Gran Paradiso, Italy. Andrew Peacock, Australia

Elephant's eye, Limpopo, South Africa. Marsel van Oosten, Netherlands

Elephants, Masai Mara, Kenya. Marsel van Oosten, Netherlands

CALL OF THE WILD

Marsel van Oosten Netherlands
Runner Up

Simply stunning and varied observations of this incredible mammal.

Elephant at waterhole, Limpopo, South Africa. Marsel van Oosten, Netherlands

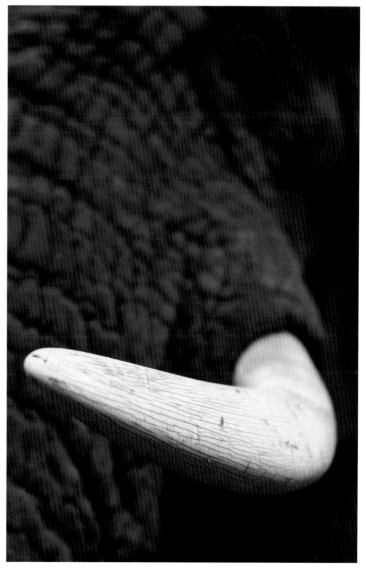

Elephant tusk, Okavango Delta, Botswana. Marsel van Oosten, Netherlands

CALL OF THE WILD

Adam Balcy Poland
Highly Commended

Adam's skyscapes have a simplicity and drama which makes them very powerful. Incredible and unusual cloud formations over wild Iceland.

Snae Fellsnes Peninsula, West Iceland. Adam Balcy, Poland

Snae Fellsnes Peninsula, West Iceland. Adam Balcy, Poland

Japanese cranes' mating ritual, Hokkaido, Japan. Simone Sbaraglia, Italy

CALL OF THE WILD

Simone Sbaraglia Italy
Commended

Simone has captured majestic moments of elaborate symmetry in a set of very elegant images.

Japanese cranes' mating ritual, Hokkaido, Japan. Simone Sbaraglia, Italy

JOY OF TRAVEL PORTFOLIO 2008

The judges chose not to give a winner's award in this category as, although there were many outstanding images entered, no single entrant effectively conveyed the joy of travel theme consistently throughout a portfolio. The three strongest entries were all Commended and the images on this and the following pages are taken from those Commended portfolios.

Sponsors of this award:

Adobe, Intrepid Travel, Lee Filters, Lexar, TPOTY, Wacom

Maasai, Corner Baridi, Kenya. Chris Minihane, USA

Seaside Park, New Jersey, USA - Fourth of July. Donna Connor, USA

Musician, Charles Bridge, Prague, Czech Republic. Donna Connor, USA

Dai Sai village, Loei,Thailand. Gavin Gough, UK

Dai Sai village, Loei,Thailand. Gavin Gough, UK

JOY OF TRAVEL

Gavin Gough UK
Commended

Gavin's joyful, intimate portraits have a relaxed charm.

JOY OF TRAVEL

Donna Connor USA
Commended

Donna's images have a fantastic sense of fun, making them very engaging.

JOY OF TRAVEL

Chris Minihane USA
Commended

A wonderful interpretation of the category theme. Chris's images also capture the vastness and adventure of the destination.

Magaidi, Kenya near the Tanzanian border. Chris Minihane, USA

ONE SHOT 2008

Destination Anywhere: Italian photographer Massimo Cristaldi's breathtakingly poignant image of Ground Zero left the judges speechless with its simplicity and serene depiction of such a tragic destination.

Sponsors of this award:

Adobe, Lexar, TPOTY

Ground Zero, New York, USA. Massimo Cristaldi, Italy

Salt lake, Salar de Uyuni, Bolivia. Jon Crane, UK

DESTINATION ANYWHERE

Jon Crane UK
Runner Up

The sheer emptiness of this image makes it enticing.

DESTINATION ANYWHERE

Massimo Cristaldi Italy
Winner

Born in Catania, Italy, Massimo Cristaldi first discovered photography at the age of 12, thanks to his father. To this day, Massimo still sometimes uses his father's FED4 camera. He has always been fascinated by photographs and images, and grew up in a house filled with sculptures, paintings and traces of the past.

A self-taught photographer, over the years he has strived to express himself through photography, creating exhibitions, and working for private customers. His images have been published online and in magazines.

Avenue of Baobabs, Madasgar. Marsel van Oosten, Netherlands

DESTINATION ANYWHERE

Marsel van Oosten Netherlands
Highly Commended

Beautifully composed and timed, Marsel's image epitomises the theme perfectly.

DESTINATION ANYWHERE

Martin Smith UK
Commended

An enchanting pastel image of man and nature.

Tavurvur volcano, Papua New Guinea. Martin Smith, UK

FIRST SHOT 2008

Wish You Were Here: 2008 saw the introduction of a new category designed to encourage and support photographers who are newer to this passion and not yet so accomplished. The First Shot category is for less experienced photographers who are still learning their craft. The judges chose the ten winners as entrants whose images show the potential to develop their photography and who would benefit from the tuition on offer as their prize.

Sponsors of this award:
Iridius, Photo Iconic, Pixfizz, TPOTY

Island of Ouvea, New Caledonia. Tristan Hewat, Australia

Champagne Ridge, near Nairobi, Kenya. Chris Minihane, USA

Skyline at night from Circular Quay, Sydney, Australia. Colm Hanratty, Ireland

Cape fur seal with sardines, Kwazulu Natal, South Africa. Iain Blair, New Zealand

Salar de Uyuni, Bolivia. Ben King, Sweden

WISH YOU WERE HERE

Winners

Ben King Sweden

Chris Minihane USA

Colm Hanratty Ireland

Ekaterina Ryabova Russia

Firas Abussaud Saudi Arabia

Iain Blair New Zealand

Michelle Bromham UK

Nadia Stone UK

Ron Sutton UK

Tristan Hewat Australia

Lake Chuzengi, Japan. Ron Sutton, UK

Botanical Garden, Mauritius. Firas Abussaud, Saudi Arabia

Mont Blanc, France. Michelle Bromham, UK

Sahara Desert, Morocco. Nadia Stone, UK

Tea room, Stratford on Avon, England. Ekaterina Ryabova, Russia

BEST SINGLE IMAGE
IN PORTFOLIO 2008

Each year there are many portfolio entries which don't win prizes but which contain outstanding individual images. In 2008 Travel Photographer of the Year introduced this award at the request of the judges to give recognition to such images. This award can be given for each portfolio category and winners are chosen by the judging panel, with further images of note awarded a special mention.

Sponsors of this award:
TPOTY

Probiscis monkey, Borneo, Malaysia. Felix Hug, Switzerland

Village elder, near Lake Bunyonyoi, Uganda. Philip Lee Harvey, UK

LIFE

Philip Lee Harvey UK
Winner

Wow! Philip's image, like all great portraits, won't let you look anywhere else. The ambiguity of whether the man's expression is joyous or intimidating adds an extra element of intrigue.

Namaqua chameleon, Namib Desert, Namibia. Marsel van Oosten, Netherlands

CALL OF THE WILD

Felix Hug Switzerland
Winner

The subtlety of this photograph and the timing and technique
required to capture it make this image a strong winner.

Marsel van Oosten Netherlands
Special Mention

Great shot giving us a glimpse of a wild moment which
happens in a fraction of a second.

Sue Flood UK
Special Mention

Simply an incredible moment and insight into this underwater
world and symbiotic interaction.

Whale calf and remora, Tonga. Sue Flood, UK

TRAVEL PHOTOGRAPHER
OF THE YEAR 2007

The startling simplicity of Cat Vinton's portfolios and the clever use of the panoramic format make her an eye-catching winner of the 2007 awards. In this part of a personal project on nomadic life, Cat incorporates elements of both documentary and fashion photography to great effect.

Sponsors of this award:

Adobe, Plastic Sandwich, Travel Photographer of the Year

Finnmark Plateau, northern Norway. Cat Vinton, UK

Sami girl running on the snow, Finnmark Plateau, northern Norway. Cat Vinton, UK

TRAVEL PHOTOGRAPHER
OF THE YEAR 2007

Cat Vinton UK
Winner

After graduating from Camberwell School of Art and Design in 1997, Cat Vinton worked as a freelance photographer in the People's Democratic Republic of Lao, working for the United Nations, UNICEF and Redd Barna, amongst others. Now based in London, she travels all over the world as a freelance photographer, shooting personal projects for exhibitions and commercially for clients.

Since she was a small girl, she has treasured imagery. She was lucky enough to live in a village amongst three 'old-school' documentary photographers, Michael Ward, Brian Wharton and Christopher Angeloglou. They inspired her enormously, and helped her to buy her first Nikon.

Husky driving, Finnmark Plateau, northern Norway. Cat Vinton, UK

Finnmark Plateau, northern Norway. Cat Vinton, UK

Yurt, Mongolia. Cat Vinton, UK

Nomad family, Mongolia. Cat Vinton, UK

Nomad family, Mongolia. Cat Vinton, UK

Nomad family, Mongolia. Cat Vinton, UK

YOUNG TRAVEL PHOTOGRAPHER
OF THE YEAR 2007

Fragile Earth: In her portfolio 14 year old Canadian photographer Luna Malka contrasts natural beauty, decay and man's use and misuse of the earth's natural resources. Her images have a graphic quality and give an interesting and youthful perspective on the highly topical issue of our environment.

Sponsors of this award:

Adobe, Adventure Ecology, Plastic Sandwich, TPOTY, Wacom

'Walking on the world' - foot and asphalt in Laval, Quebec, Canada. Luna Malka, Canada

Polluted lake in Laval, Quebec, Canada. Luna Malka, Canada

'Glitter or litter?' - streamers from outdoor party in Toronto, Canada. Luna Malka, Canada

YOUNG TRAVEL PHOTOGRAPHER
OF THE YEAR 2007

Luna Malka Canada
Winner

Luna Malka is the third generation in a family of photographers scattered over the globe. She has been taking photographs since a young age, traveling to Europe and the United States and shooting with her father's Elph film camera.

In late 2006, she received a Panasonic Lumix digital camera and began taking it everywhere with her, shooting portraits of her friends, cityscapes, street scenes, landscapes and nature. Luna was just 14 years old when she won Young TPOTY.

'Green peace' - plant, Quebec, Canada. Luna Malka, Canada

ONE PLANET MANY LIVES
PORTFOLIO 2007

Timothy Allen's portfolio from Northern India and Bhutan provides an insight into lives filled with colour, formality and tradition. Amidst the order we see glimpses of outside influences which both enhance and threaten the native culture.

Sponsors of this award:

Adobe, HP, Intrepid Travel, JP Distribution, Lee Filters

Bru Tribal Dance, Tripura, India. Timothy Allen, UK

Monks and MacBook, Simtokha Dzong, Bhutan. Timothy Allen, UK

ONE PLANET MANY LIVES

Timothy Allen UK
Winner

In the 1990s, after beginning a part-time diploma in photography at Hereford College of Art and Design, Timothy Allen joined an aid convoy to Bosnia in order to shoot his first year reportage project. Six months later he had left college, moved to London and begun working for the Sunday Telegraph, later undertaking commissions from all the British broadsheet publications and finally a six year position at The Independent, working predominantly on features and portraits.

In recent years, the focus of his work has turned to the planet's remaining tribal societies and he devotes his time to documenting the diversity of humanity's cultural heritage. He has worked with indigenous communities throughout the world, most extensively in India and South East Asia.

Timothy's work has been included in countless books and exhibitions.

Women queuing to receive blessing, Thimpu Dzong, Bhutan. Timothy Allen, UK

Ao Naga tribe, Nagaland, North East India. Timothy Allen, UK

Tibetan Worship. Larry Louie, Canada

Tibetan Worship. Larry Louie, Canada

Tibetan Worship. Larry Louie, Canada

ONE PLANET MANY LIVES

Larry Louie Canada
Runner Up

Masterfully crafted black and white images give Larry's
subjects a strong presence and a context to their lives.

Tibetan Worship. Larry Louie, Canada

Kaunas, Lithuania. Gary Wornell, Finland

Kaunas, Lithuania. Gary Wornell, Finland

ONE PLANET MANY LIVES

Gary Wornell Finland
Highly Commended

Gritty urban life and bold composition characterise Gary's portfolio.

Two children in window, Kham, Tibet. Jean-Claude Louis, USA

ONE PLANET MANY LIVES

Jean-Claude Louis USA
Commended

Jean-Claude's character studies of Tibetan children have an enchanting quality.

Nomad girl, Amdo, Tibet. Jean-Claude Louis, USA

SENSE OF PLACE
PORTFOLIO 2007

A hauntingly simple yet refreshingly different view of Berlin caught the eye of the judges to win the Sense of Place portfolio award for American photographer, Jean-Claude Louis. The atmosphere is palpable.

Sponsors of this award:

Adobe, African Safari Roots, JP Distribution, Lee Filters, Wacom

Alexanderplatz, Berlin, Germany. Jean-Claude Louis, USA

Remnants of wall, Berlin, Germany. Jean-Claude Louis, USA

SENSE OF PLACE

Jean-Claude Louis USA
Winner

Born in Alsace, France, Jean-Claude Louis moved to Southern California in 1990. A physician and scientist, he had a lengthy career in biomedical research, which he left in 2007 to pursue his two passions, travel and photography.

His work is largely rooted in cultural, social and ecological issues. He has travelled to more than forty countries in five continents, creating images that explore people, their culture and their relationship with their environment.

Commune, Oranienburgerstrasse, Berlin, Germany. Jean-Claude Louis, USA

Hill of Crosses, Siaulai, Lithuania. Philippe Gueissaz, Switzerland

SENSE OF PLACE

Philippe Gueissaz Switzerland
Runner Up

An eerie chill makes Philippe's portfolio all the more atmospheric and enigmatic.

Hill of Crosses, Siaulai, Lithuania. Philippe Gueissaz, Switzerland

Hill of Crosses, Siaulai, Lithuania. Philippe Gueissaz, Switzerland

Hill of Crosses, Siaulai, Lithuania. Philippe Gueissaz, Switzerland

Atop the Empire State Building, USA. Ashok Sinha, USA/India

SENSE OF PLACE

Ashok Sinha USA/India
Highly Commended

Ashok has clearly shown how the simple and familiar can
still convey a sense of mood and place.

Atop the Empire State Building, USA. Ashok Sinha, USA/India

SENSE OF PLACE

Luke Duggleby UK

Commended

Simple images, well shot, speak volumes about the horrors
and inhumanity of this place.

THRILL PORTFOLIO 2007

The sheer insignificance of man's presence in such a vast and unforgiving landscape adds to the sense of the thrill of venturing into it. Moody, atmospheric and inspiring images beautifully captured in black and white by Polish photographer, Maciej Duczynski.

Sponsors of this award:

Adobe, Fujifilm, JP Distribution, Lee Filters, Yokmok Adventures

Tatra Mountains, Poland. Maciej Duczynski, Poland

Mountains, Western Norway. Maciej Duczynski, Poland

THRILL

Maciej Duczynski Poland
Winner

Born in Katowice, in the south of Poland in 1975, Maciej discovered his passion for travelling while studying at Technical University in Gliwice. After a few years the second passion - photography - followed.

He specialises in landscape photography and prefers the cold beauty and wilderness of northern Scandinavia. Maciej exhibits his photographs in Poland and writes articles about landscape photography and post-processing of digital images for various European photo magazines.

Landsmannalaugar, Iceland. Maciej Duczynski, Poland

Parasailing, Pantai Cenang, Langkawi, Malaysia. Felix Hug, Switzerland

THRILL

Felix Hug Switzerland
Runner Up

With varied and uplifting images, Felix captures the pleasure
and excitement of the locations he photographed.

Chocolate Hills, Bohol, Philippines. Felix Hug, Switzerland

Yi Peng Festival, Chiang Mai, Thailand. Felix Hug, Switzerland

Sunrise, Borobodur, Indonesia. Felix Hug, Switzerland

La Tomatina, Spain. Andrew Watson, Australia

THRILL

Andrew Watson Australia
Highly Commended

Andrew's Tomatina images encapsulate the thrill, fun and sheer joyous mess of the event.

La Tomatina, Spain. Andrew Watson, Australia

Pamplona, Spain. James Hill, UK

THRILL

James Hill UK
Commended

Great use of perspective and viewpoint make James's images
engaging, thrilling and thought provoking.

Pamplona, Spain. James Hill, UK

ONE SHOT 2007

Special Places, Amazing Faces: Breaking all the rules of composition, Richard Murai's image draws you into the life of this 84 year old Cambodian snail gatherer. This is her world, and every bit of it is etched on her amazing face.

Sponsors of this award:

Adobe, JP Distribution, Lee Filters, TPOTY

Snail gatherer, Tonle Sap Lake, Cambodia. Richard Murai, USA

SPECIAL PLACES, AMAZING FACES

Richard Murai USA
Winner

Born, raised and educated in the San Francisco Bay Area, Richard Murai now teaches creative photography in Northern California's Central Valley. His ongoing fascination with documenting sacred sites of the world has generated travel to locations within India, Peru, Turkey, Egypt, Russia, Asia and Western Europe.

SPECIAL PLACES, AMAZING FACES

Tony Baker UK
Runner Up

An awe-inspiring image of an awe-inspiring place.

Entrance to Di Feng Dong, Sichuan, China. Tony Baker, UK

Tengger horseman, Mount Bromo, Java, Indonesia. Larry Louie, Canada

SPECIAL PLACES, AMAZING FACES

Larry Louie Canada
Highly Commended

Larry's sense for unusual composition makes this image all
the more striking in all its wonderland detail.

Faces, Turkey. Robert Moore, UK

SPECIAL PLACES,
AMAZING FACES

Robert Moore UK
Commended

Great composition and an engaging 'amazing' face made
Robert's image a strong contender.

'Halo' – Paris, France. Leslie Rosenthal, USA

SPECIAL PLACES, AMAZING FACES

Leslie Rosenthal, USA
Commended

High contrast creates a haunting quality to an enchanting image.

NEW TALENT 2007

Insight: 2007 saw the introduction of the first Travel Photographer of the Year award for new and emerging talent, with the objective of helping to launch the career of an up and coming photographer. Although this award was designed to reward potential, Charlie Mahoney's winning images are reasonably accomplished for a relative newcomer to photography, showing early ability to observe and tell a story through imagery.

Sponsors of this award:

Adobe, Adventure Ecology, Iridius, Plastic Sandwich, TPOTY

Girls selling fruit, Burkina Faso. Charlie Mahoney, USA.

Prague, Czech Republic. Charlie Mahoney, USA

NEW TALENT

Charlie Mahoney USA
Winner

Following a 15-year career in finance and investment, Charlie Mahoney completed a Master's in Photojournalism at the Universidat Autonoma de Barcelona in July 2006. The following month he began a three-month trip through Benin, Burkina Faso and Togo. He has subsequently traveled to St. Bart's in the French West Indies, Prague, Albania, Montenegro and Corfu, Greece.

Charlie strongly believes that photojournalism can promote change by functioning as a witness and giving a voice to people who are powerless to tell their own stories.

Barcelona, Spain. Charlie Mahoney, USA

Boy with ball, Maine, USA. Charlie Mahoney, USA

BEST OF THE REST

Every year the TPOTY team is privileged to view many, many thousands of images from photographers across the world, showing every aspect of travel. And every year, amongst those images, there are some which really catch our eye. We could easily fill a dozen books with such photographs, giving recognition to some truly deserving photographers and giving a great deal of pleasure to readers.

However, within the context of this book we have limited space, so we had to make some very difficult decisions and leave out some truly magnificent images. What follows over the next few pages is a selection of photographs which, although not amongst the winners, are particular favourites of the Travel Photographer of the Year team.

We hope you enjoy them as much as we do.

Font Magica, Barcelona, Spain. Olivia Rutherford, UK

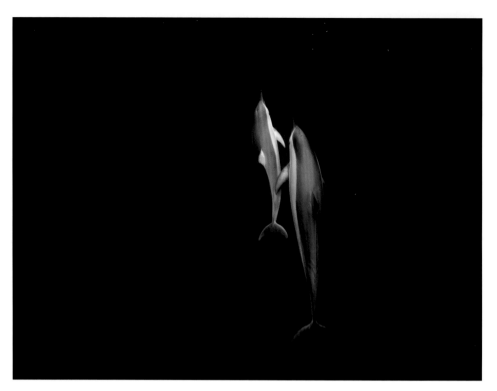

Dolphins, Kona, Hawaii, USA. Ryan Hellard, Canada

Road crossing, Tokyo, Japan. Jose Mosquera, Spain

Bell's Cafe, Broken Hill, New South Wales, Australia. Felix Hug, Switzerland

Festival de la Virgen del Carmen, Pisac, Peru. Richard Murai, USA

UNESCO World Heritage Site, Shirakawa-go, Gifu, Japan. Shannon Donnelly, USA

Xing Ping, Southern China. Simon Morris, UK

Shogun trail in the cedar forests at Hakone, Japan. Charles McKean, Australia

Bull elephant, Masai Mara Game Reserve, Kenya. Angela Scott, Kenya

Monks watching Tsechu festival,Thimphu,Bhutan. Jim Stephens, UK

Flautist in American marching band, Dublin, Ireland. Vincent Long, Australia

Parallel Lives, Varanasi, India. Gavin Gough, UK

Tuareg tribe camel race, Tamanrasset, Algeria. Frans Lemmens, Netherlands

Man on train tracks, Kashi, India. Greg Vore, USA

Theystareykir Terma Area, Fumarole, Iceland. Sergey Rumyantsev, Russia

Polar bear mother and cubs, Svalbard, Norway. Dennis Bromage, UK

Smiling for the camera, St Lucia, Caribbean. Emily Butters, UK

THE JUDGES

TPOTY judging panels are made up of experts from the worlds of photography and travel. The panel is selected to reflect a variety of backgrounds, styles and attitudes to photography and the photographic image. A key element of the panel is the wealth of visual and technical expertise brought into the mix by our technical and creative judges.

Lay judges and past winners of these awards have also participated, bringing fresh ideas and perspectives to the judging process.

These judges give their time because they love photography, and we are immensely grateful for their efforts and support.

We would like to thank the following, who have featured on some (or all) of the 2007, 2008 and 2009 judging panels:

Andrew James – editor, Practical Photography

Avril O'Reilly – picture editor, Daily Telegraph Travel

Ben Mallalieu – travel writer, Guardian

Brigitte Lardinois – special projects director, Magnum Photos

Caroline Metcalfe – director of photography, Condé Nast Traveller

Chris Coe – photographer, author and lecturer

Chris Weston – award winning wildlife photographer and author

Colin Findlay – head of World Illustrated at photoshot.com

Debbie Ireland – picture editor and former
head of AA World Picture Library

Erin Moroney – head of Axiom photographic agency

Georg Gerster – pioneer aerial photographer

Ian Farrell – editor, Professional Photographer

Jeremy Hoare – travel photographer, TV
cameraman and lighting expert, writer

Manfred Zollner – editor, fotoMAGAZIN, Germany

Mark Bannister – digital and film retoucher

Melinda Stevens – travel editor, Tatler

Melissa De Witt – editor, HotShoe International magazine

Nick Meers – landscape and panoramic
photographer, author and lecturer

Simon Bainbridge – editor, British Journal of Photography

Terry Steeley – digital imaging expert

SPONSORS

Adobe

The Adobe® Photoshop® family of products is the ultimate playground for bringing out the best in your digital images. Using Adobe Photoshop Lightroom 2 for developing images, together with Adobe Photoshop CS4 for retouching, digital photographers now have the complete and essential photography software toolkit.

www.adobe.com   www.adobe.com/products/photoshop/family/

Connekt Colour

Connekt Colour, the print division of the Technik group, delivers brilliant print and faultless, calm, untroubled service. Continual investment in technology and people allows Connekt to respond to the needs of its clients. Whatever the message, however complex the job, however difficult or unusual the treatment, Connekt meets the challenge. Connekt Colour prints the Travel Photographer of the Year portfolio books - Journey One, Journey Two and Journey Three.

www.connektcolour.com

HARMAN/ILFORD

HARMAN technology Ltd

HARMAN technology Limited is a pioneering professional imaging specialist based in the UK. It maintains three, separate, well-known brands. ILFORD PHOTO manufactures traditional monochrome photographic products, including the full range of film, paper and chemistry. HARMAN PHOTO produces a range of high-end inkjet papers featuring a real photo Fibre Baryta base giving true photographic weight and feel, with outstanding image quality in terms of extensive colour gamut, excellent tones and archival permanence properties, suitable for both colour and monochrome prints. Also, HARMAN CRYSTALJET Resin Coated paper designed to produce quick drying, high quality photo images on popular photo-dedicated inkjet printers using dye or pigment inks. KENTMERE PHOTOGRAPHIC produces a range of black and white photographic products and wide format inkjet display media.

www.ilfordphoto.com   www.harman-inkjet.com   www.kentmere.com

Intrepid Travel

Travelling the Intrepid way means exploring the world with a small group of likeminded travellers. Joining locals on their trains, in their villages and even in their homes, you'll see and photograph more than just the usual sites, you'll become a part of local life. Whether it's a river journey on the Mekong, a Peruvian trek, an Italian feast or an African safari, Intrepid takes travellers to every continent from 2010 and has adventures to suit just about every budget and comfort level. Intrepid are proud to support the Journeys series, and we would love to show you our favourite corners of the world.

www.intrepidtravel.com

Jacobs Digital Photo & Video

Jacobs Digital Photo & Video continues to develop as the United Kingdom's largest independent photographic retailer by its their reach from Edinburgh to London with 18 stores nationwide. Offering unrivalled service, choice and value for the serious photographer, Jacobs stands out in the Digital SLR and compact camera marketplace. We also cater for the video and optic enthusiast with a wide range of camcorders, binoculars and accessories. The company ethos has been structured around customer service and professionalism for over 75 years and our specially trained staff in every store are committed to satisfying every customer's needs.

www.jacobsdigital.co.uk

LEE Filters

There is a reason why LEE Filters has established a worldwide reputation for quality that is second to none. It is because every filter that leaves the factory has been handmade and inspected by one of our highly skilled staff, who ensures it will meet our exacting standards. This rigorous process and attention to detail at every level means that LEE Filters has, since its inception in 1978, been assured of its position as the benchmark in camera filters – its status backed up by the many photographers worldwide who continue to recommend its products for both film and digital photography.

www.leefilters.com

Lexar Media

Lexar Media, Inc. boasts one of the most comprehensive offerings of memory product lines in the industry. We deliver high-quality, award-winning products in every memory category: USB flash drives, all popular form factors of memory cards and card readers, DRAM computer memory for PCs and Mac systems, and solid state drives (SSD). We back our products with outstanding customer support and industry-leading warranties, and we strive to expand our offerings to meet the ever-changing needs of our customers. The Lexar brand has long been synonymous with reliable, high-performance products, which is reflected in the award-winning memory products and USB flash drives sold under the Lexar name.

www.lexar.com

Travel Photographer of the Year would also like to thank African Safari Roots, Fujifilm, Hewlett Packard, Iridius, JP Distribution, Rough Guides and Yokmok Adventures.

Without the support of all the companies listed on this and the next page, there would be no TPOTY awards and we are hugely grateful for their input.

The Iceberg Graveyard, Pleneau Bay, Antarctic Peninsula. Jose Antonio Rosas, Peru

SPONSORS

Linhof Studio

Linhof Studio was established in 1977 as the UK importer for the Linhof range of professional photographic equipment. Over the last three decades, the company has continually expanded its product range and services to become not only a professional importer and retailer of Linhof precision cameras and Hensel lighting, but also of a comprehensive range of cameras and lighting, darkroom equipment, papers, specialised photographic film and processing chemistry. The Linhof Studio has gained a reputation for knowledge and service to help photographers make the right decisions around their equipment needs. Today, the company's aim remains to help the professional and serious enthusiast photographer select the right camera and equipment to match their needs in large and medium format work, for both analogue and digital.

www.linhofstudio.com

Mountain Paradise

Mountain Paradise specialises in holidays to the High Tatras in Slovakia, an unspoilt mountain range in one of the most beautiful undiscovered areas in the heart of Europe. We offer an extensive range of quality package holidays in the Tatra Mountains, which can be individually tailor made for you. And we have teamed up with renowned British professional photographers to bring you one of the most scenic photography landscape workshops in the heart of Europe. The region has everything a photographer could wish for: unique culture, historical architecture, friendly people and, of course, spectacular landscapes. We aim to cater for everyone's needs. What puts us above the rest is that we pride ourselves on customer satisfaction and the personal service we offer to everyone who travels with us. This will be your most memorable mountain holiday in Europe, which will make you want to return year after year.

www.mountainparadise.co.uk

NEC

Empowered by Innovation **NEC**

NEC is a world leading, trusted Display Manufacturer from Japan. Enjoy unparalleled display performance in your colour-critical applications with SpectraViewII Series LCD displays from NEC Display Solutions. All processing stages, from receiving or scanning a picture to printing, can take place on the screen, resulting in more than 90 percent of all decisions regarding colour presentation being made on the monitor itself. Thus choosing the optimal display is key to the success of your colour critical workflow. NEC SpectraView's outstanding features and benefits for best picture quality and colour accuracy, outstanding ergonomics and amazing value for money provide the perfect prerequisites for colour-critical image processing, be it for digital photography, pre-press or high-performance graphic design and video animation applications.

www.nec-display-solutions.co.uk

Photo Iconic

Photo Iconic offers a range of photography workshops, courses, masterclasses and international adventures to suit all abilities and styles of photography - all tutored by award-winning photographers. We specialise in hands-on practical and pragmatic tuition presented in a clear and concise way and our objective is to help you improve your photography. All courses are fully tutored and we spend our time helping you, not shooting our own images. Tuition includes camera craft, photographic technique, creative image making, image editing, shooting to sell, the business of photography and much more. Whether you're a beginner, a keen amateur or have turned professional, whether you use a digital camera or shoot film, whether you take landscape photographs, people, travel or wildlife photography, we can help you to make better photographs.

www.photoiconic.com

Pixfizz

Pixfizz is the ideal solution for all photographers as it can add value to your work whether you are an amateur or a seasoned professional. With a range of flexible features such as your own gallery design and site hosting options there is always a cost-effective solution available whatever your needs.

www.pixfizz.com

Plastic Sandwich

Plastic Sandwich has been building portfolios for photographers and art directors since the early 1970s. It was founded and is still run by Joyce Pinto and Rob Jacobs - who's been with the company for 30 years. Between them they have unparalleled experience in this field. Plastic Sandwich has clients all over the world; wherever there is a photographic industry. They include household names and stars of the industry, plus assistants and students, who find the advice the company can offer of great help. Our services are also utilised by companies such as event organisers, PR organisations - anyone whose activities or craft are best shown through the presentation of images.

www.plasticsandwich.co.uk

Wacom

Wacom's vision to bring people and technology closer together through natural interface technologies has made it the world's leading manufacturer of pen tablets, interactive pen displays, and digital interface solutions. The advanced technology of Wacom's intuitive input devices has been used to create some of the most exciting digital art, films, special effects, fashion and designs around the world and provides business and home users with leading interface technology to express their personality.

www.wacom.eu

Man filming dancers at Toka festival, Tanna Island, Vanuatu. Jonathan Clay, UK